Original title:
Bows and Beginnings

Copyright © 2025 Creative Arts Management OÜ
All rights reserved.

Author: Fiona Harrington
ISBN HARDBACK: 978-1-80586-036-5
ISBN PAPERBACK: 978-1-80586-508-7

The First Embrace

In a world so wobbly and round,
Two friends were lost, nowhere to be found.
They topped a hill, their hearts all aflutter,
Then stumbled down, right into the butter!

They giggled and rolled, what a silly scene,
With laughter so loud, like a movie screen.
They formed a pact, to always be near,
With smudged up faces, they cracked up in cheer.

With jelly and jam, they painted the sky,
And flew kites made of old laundry ties.
A silly remark, a tickle, a race,
Their friendship began with a laugh and a chase.

So here's to the falls, the jars that we break,
To the mess we create, and the smiles we make.
For life's just a game, with giggles and spins,
And the best kind of start, is where laughter begins.

The Fabric of First Steps

In a world of clumsy dance,
A toddler's wiggle, not a chance.
Shoes on wrong, the laces tight,
But laughter sparkles in the night.

With each tiny, exaggerated fall,
They bounce back up, and giggle, y'all.
The early stumbles turning heads,
As cat-like grace soon spreads, not dreads.

Resilient Threads

Life's a weave of mischief bright,
Where tangled yarn can bring delight.
A sock goes missing, who can tell?
It's tied a knot, inside its shell.

With every snag, a new tale spins,
Of crafty socks, and silly wins.
Each twist and loop, a hearty cheer,
Worn with pride, no sock left sheer.

Colors of a New Dawn

In morning hues, a splendid sight,
With paint on faces, laughter's flight.
Crayon scribbles on the wall,
Who needs a canvas? Not at all!

A wild parade of mismatched socks,
Funky colors, shifting clocks.
Sunshine peeks through curtains drawn,
As giggles echo with a yawn.

The Loop of Opportunity

Round and round, the circle flies,
An endless ride beneath the skies.
With each brave jump, a chance to grin,
As joy unfolds, let the fun begin.

Chasing dreams on roller skates,
Falling down, oh, what a fate!
Yet laughter lingers, bright and clear,
As every turn brings us near.

The Journey Unfurled

With a map that's upside down,
We set out with quite a frown.
Left shoes on the right feet,
Oh, this adventure's quite a treat!

We spied a goat wearing a hat,
Played hide and seek with a cat.
Bumps and bruises, laughter and cheer,
Every misstep brings us near!

Caress of the Unknown

In a forest of jellybean trees,
We dance with squirrels, if you please.
A raccoon's your partner in crime,
He steals your snacks, oh what fun time!

With each twist, a giggle erupts,
Who knew that life would disrupt?
Unplanned trips lead to delight,
Imperfect plans feel so right!

New Ties in the Breeze

Kites tangled in the branches sway,
Each turn leads us further astray.
We trip over shoelaces tight,
Laughing hard, what a funny sight!

New pals made in the funniest ways,
Through puddles we jump, a wild phase.
Chasing dreams with paper planes,
Life's a circus, no one complains!

A Dance with the Unseen

The wind whispers secrets so sly,
We twirl round and round, oh me, oh my!
Invisible partners lead us astray,
But who needs sight when you're this giddy?

Steps are skipped, laughter spills wide,
As we stumble, we giggle with pride.
Falling over a garden gnome,
We find ourselves, still far from home!

Embracing the Unknown

In a world of twists and turns,
We dance like socks that never match.
With each step, the laughter churns,
In the joke of fate, we find our catch.

We wear confusion like a crown,
Trip over dreams, oh what a sight!
But when we tumble, never frown,
For every fall feels rather light.

Knots of Potential

Tangled thoughts play hide and seek,
Like spaghetti on a daring night.
Each twist reveals what we can tweak,
Just laugh it off — it feels just right!

In a jumble, we forge anew,
Creating paths that make us grin.
With every knot, a spark will brew,
Who knew chaos could help us win?

Horizons Yet to Discover

With maps drawn in crayon and cheer,
We set out on this wobbly ride.
The iconic signs all disappear,
But what a thrill to just collide!

Each horizon laughs with glee,
As we skip over rocks and streams.
Who cares about a cup of tea?
We're brewing up the biggest dreams!

The First Light of Possibility

Morning giggles wake the sun,
With silly hats and goofy grins.
Every chance feels like pure fun,
As we foxtrot through our whims.

With eyes wide open to the day,
We bounce like balls across the floor.
In this mischief, come what may,
The first light shines on dreams galore!

Whispers of a Fresh Start

In winter's chill, we trip and tumble,
Yet spring arrives, with giggles and grumble.
New socks slip off, on lawns we tumble,
We wave at the sun, with a silly mumble.

The cat walks by in her finest hat,
While I tie my shoes, and fall flat.
Laughter erupts, like a bubbling brew,
A fresh start is messy, but oh-so-true!

Ribbons of Dawn

A rooster crows, with a hesitant squawk,
I fumble for coffee, while socks go for a walk.
The sun peeks in, with a wink and a nudge,
While my cereal dances, water fights the grudge.

Jumping at dreams, like fish on a line,
Sipping sweet chaos, like it's all perfectly fine.
In this wacky morning where mishaps reign,
Every sip of joy makes the laughter regain!

The Ties That Unravel

With shoes untied and hair like hay,
I chase my friend down the bumpy way.
We tumble and giggle, hands over our eyes,
Each stumble a treasure, each laugh a surprise.

The world's a jigsaw, pieces askew,
But hey, who's counting when we're me and you?
Ribbons of nonsense, we tie with delight,
In a game of tomfoolery, life's full of light!

A Dance of New Horizons

Under blue skies, we pirouette fast,
A merry-go-round of moments amassed.
With hiccups and snickers, we leap and we spin,
Life's silly dance, let the laughter begin!

From horizon to horizon, we twirl and we sway,
Making fools of ourselves, come what may.
A toast to the clumsy, the awkward, the wise,
In the grand ballet, it's joy that we prize!

Embracing the Unknotted Horizon

A cat in a hat tips over,
Chasing its tail with glee.
With strings of fate all twisted,
Who knows what we might see?

A dance on a new tightrope,
Wobbling with a goofy grin.
Life's a game of silly toss,
Where mishaps begin to spin.

Colors splash like paintballs,
A canvas made of laughs.
Each stumble a funny memory,
In our joyful craft.

A leap into the unknown,
With laughter as our guide.
We'll untangle the weird pathways,
And wear them with pride.

Hues of New Beginnings

The sun peeks through the curtains,
A rooster's old alarm clock shrieks.
Waking all the sleepy dreams,
With colors bold and cheeky squeaks.

The toaster pops a crumply tune,
While breakfast dances in the pan.
Each bite could bring a chuckle,
Delightful chaos—oh, what a plan!

An upturned coffee mug rolls,
Spilling laughter on the floor.
We laugh at the little blunders,
This is what fun is for!

With every spilled or dropped toast,
We toast to life with cheer.
Each morning's a bright canvas,
Smudged with love and a sneer.

The Arch of Tomorrow

A rubber band snaps loudly,
Sending notes across the room.
A paper airplane takes a flight,
In chaotic, joyful bloom.

Jumping jacks in mismatched socks,
With giggles filling the air.
Tomorrow wears a silly hat,
And whirls without a care.

We paint our future lightly,
With splashes of love and mirth.
Each color burst—an echo,
Of laughter's joyful worth.

So let's embrace tomorrows,
And tie them in a bow,
With fun and silly antics,
As we ride this wacky flow.

Tied With Hope

A long string of silly stories,
Knotty tales wrapped tight with dreams.
Each twist an unexpected jolt,
Of laughter bursting at the seams.

A balloon floats past the window,
Squeaking with each little pounce.
It carries hopes and wishes,
And suggests a joyful bounce.

With every thread of fate we pull,
A giggle crosses the line.
We keep our spirits soaring high,
And let the sunshine shine.

So here's to all the surprises,
Life's mischief, let it cope.
Each laugh a gentle nudge,
That keeps us tied with hope.

The Archer's Heart

An archer stood with a grin,
His target missed, he laughed within.
The arrow flew, a wild spree,
It hit the tree, oh woe is me!

With every shot, a giggle would rise,
He aimed for glory, but what a surprise.
The squirrels watched with popcorn in hand,
As arrows danced, a miss was grand!

He sharpened his skills with every 'whoops!',
Turning mishaps into giggling loops.
His quiver filled with dreams so bright,
Each fail a story, a true delight.

Through laughter's bow, his spirit soared,
In the art of jest, he was adored.
For every aim that went astray,
He'd shoot again, to save the day!

Ribbons of Renewal

In a world tied up with shiny strings,
A ribbon dance, oh the joy it brings.
Each slip and slide, a new surprise,
Tangled dreams and twinkling eyes.

With every knot, a giggle burst,
Oh look at this! A ribbon cursed!
They flapped and flailed, a colorful sight,
Twisting and twirling, a pure delight.

The ribbons stretched from here to there,
They caught the breeze and danced in the air.
A simple tug brought laughter anew,
As colors swirled in a joyful hue.

In life's great bow, the laughter twirled,\nRenewed their spirits, the ribbons swirled.
With every twist, a memory made,
In moments of fun, their worries swayed.

Stringing Together Dreams

With string in hand, a plan was laid,
A dream weaver's thread, adventures played.
But oh dear me, a tangle ensued,
What once was neat, now misconstrued.

Each loop a whim, a giggling chase,
As dreams escaped, they set the pace.
They raced and rolled, in loops of glee,
From tangled mess to pure jubilee.

"Let's tie it here!" they'd shout and cheer,
With every knot, the laughter near.
The dreams entwined like a silly dance,
In mischief's grip, they took a chance.

In quirky threads, their hearts would gleam,
Stringing the chaos, crafting a dream.
For in the jumbles, joy could be found,
With playful hearts, their laughter resound.

Arched Horizons

Beneath the arches where the sun did play,
A band of jesters brightened the day.
They leaped and pranced, with bows held high,
Their laughter echoed; they reached for the sky.

Each arch a story, each giggle a line,
As whimsical creatures danced in a line.
The horizon beckoned, with all its charms,
In fits of fun, they spun in arms.

From rising sun to a setting hue,
Their joy unfurled as courage grew.
With every arc, new tales were spun,
In silly stunts, they found their fun.

So whether high or, in chaos, they play,
The arches of laughter light up the way.
With every leap and every cheer,
Their horizons grew wide, with no end near.

Cascading Invitations

A party's afoot, with cake on the floor,
The guests are arriving, and one breaks the door.
With laughter and giggles, the chaos unfolds,
As balloons float above, each story retold.

The cat wears a hat, and the dog brings a drink,
A toast to the mishaps, let's all really think.
With confetti on carpets and frosting on cheeks,
Here's to the joy that our wild meeting speaks!

The Glistening of Opportunity

A slip on a banana, a dance out of time,
The chance of a lifetime, all mixed up in rhyme.
With sparkles of laughter and hiccups galore,
We trip into futures while hopping on floor.

The clock says it's midnight, or is it a prank?
With friends in the mix, who needs any rank?
We stumble through wishes, like jesters in play,
Creating bright futures in our own silly way!

Weaving Dreams Anew

A thread of confusion, a knot here and there,
We stitch up our hopes in a patchwork of care.
With needles of laughter, we poke and we prod,
Turning mishaps to magic, we're charmingly flawed.

A tapestry dares us to twirl and to spin,
While puns weave around us, we're free to begin.
In colors of giggles, our dreams intertwine,
Sewing joy into moments, making our lives shine!

The Art of Starting Over

A spill on the canvas, a brush out of place,
We paint over blunders with splashes of grace.
With chuckles and snorts, we create something new,
A masterpiece born from the silly and true.

Each stroke tells a story, each layer a laugh,
Our art's a reflection, a quirky life graph.
So here's to the start, where the fun never ends,
With colors of joy that our humor lends!

Threads of Tomorrow

In a town where laughter sings,
Threads of dreams take to the wings.
Each twist and turn brings a smile,
Silly patterns stretch a mile.

People tangled, yarns awry,
Strutting past with goofy sighs.
With each knot, a tale is spun,
Creating joy, oh what a fun!

Colors clash but spirits lift,
As they gather all their gifts.
A spool of whimsy in their hands,
Crafting laughter in big bands.

Tomorrow waits with open arms,
As they dance, despite the charms.
With threads so bright, they weave the jest,
And stitch the world, a funny fest.

A New Tune Strings Along

Oh, the strings that hum and play,
Whistle tunes, come out to sway.
A ukulele, small and spry,
Resonates with every sigh.

Each pluck and strum sends giggles round,
As everyone jumps up unbound.
They dance in socks, so slippery,
To the rhythm, oh how merry!

With every note, a joke is born,
As laughter's magic is adorned.
A comedic symphony unfolds,
Turning dreams to tales retold.

Strings all twisted in delight,
Composing joys into the night.
With every laugh, a song takes flight,
A tune of fun, the heart's delight.

The Bowmaker's Craft

In a shop where bowstrings gleam,
The bowmaker crafts a dream.
Wooden arcs and tales abound,
Where humor's aim can be found.

Crafting bows with playful grace,
A wink and smile upon their face.
Each pull of string, a cheeky tease,
As giggles float upon the breeze.

The bows may twist or bend just right,
They launch the laughter into flight.
Silly targets all around,
Aiming for the joy unbound.

With every arrow, a quip takes flight,
Firing echoes into the night.
For in this place, with every craft,
Laughter is the truest draft.

Unraveling Secrets

In a world of tangled yarn,
Where secrets hide behind a barn.
Unraveling all, with guffaws loud,
Creating smiles in a crowd.

Knots that twist like silly pranks,
Hidden tales behind the thanks.
With every pull, a laugh erupts,
As tangled truths get swept up.

Colors clash and patterns play,
Every thread a new cliché.
Silly whispers fill the air,
As secrets dance without a care.

Each unravel leads to delight,
With giggles echoing through the night.
For every knot that comes apart,
A funny tale will steal the heart.

Soft Curves of Change

Life's a roundabout, quite absurd,
We trip on dreams, like flying birds.
Juggling hopes, we spin and sway,
Laughter echoing as we play.

Each twist and turn, we breathe a sigh,
Like overcooked pasta, oh me, oh my!
We stumble on paths with paint and cheer,
In this madcap dance, there's nothing to fear.

The Gift of a New Day

Woke up this morning, coffee in hand,
Surrounded by socks that never did land.
The sun takes a bow, with a wink so wide,
While my hair has chosen to run and hide.

A toast to the moments, both silly and grand,
A pancake flip-off, I don't understand!
New chances arrive, like a cat in a hat,
Spinning around, oh, imagine that!

Dance of the Future

Two left feet on a bright dance floor,
Accident-prone, I trip and soar.
With moves like a jelly and giggles abound,
I twirl to the music, perplexingly wound.

Futures unfolding in wobbly grace,
Dinner plans dashed in this dizzy race.
But laughter's the melody, keepin' it light,
In this clumsy jig, we take flight.

Curved Promises

Promises wrapped in a twisty bow,
Unraveling secrets no one could know.
Like socks in the dryer, they play hide and seek,
With playful intent, they peek and they sneak.

A hint of mischief, a touch of delight,
The weirdest of journeys, a whimsical flight.
So here's to the curves, the bends in the road,
Where even the chaos can lighten your load.

Arcs of Inspiration

In a world of laughter and play,
We leap like frogs on a sunny day.
With wobbly legs and silly grins,
Each stumble adds to the fun that win.

Colors swirl in the mind's parade,
Ideas bounce, they never fade.
In this circus of dreams and schemes,
We juggle joy, or so it seems.

A dance of quirks, a joyous sight,
We twirl around, through day and night.
Chasing giggles like a silly game,
Crafting moments that feel the same.

From hiccups that make us laugh aloud,
To goofy moves that make us proud.
In every twist, our spirits soar,
Creating arcs that crave for more.

Threads that Bind

In the web of friendship, we weave delight,
With laughter threads that shine so bright.
A kite of humor flies so high,
While wobbly strings make us comply.

We stitch together tales so wild,
With puns as fun as a carefree child.
Each loop a memory, each knot a share,
In this vibrant quilt, we dance without care.

From awkward moments to shared surprise,
We thread our hearts, a dance that flies.
With every twist, the laughter grows,
Binding us in joy, as everyone knows.

In the fabric of time, we brightly glow,
Creating patterns in the ebb and flow.
A tapestry of humor, warm and kind,
As we stitch together the threads that bind.

The Brimming Potential

Like a soda can that's just been shook,
Life's fizzy surprises are worth a look.
Each bubble pops with a spark so bright,
In every fizz, we find pure delight.

With wobbly dreams and hopeful hearts,
We soar like rockets that twirl and dart.
Potential bubbling like a joyous cheer,
Filled with laughter and silly ideas.

In the carnival of the mind's grand fair,
We ride the rollercoaster without a care.
The ups, the downs, the twists and bends,
Each giggle is a chance that never ends.

So let's embrace the quirky fate,
And celebrate the chances we create.
For in this carnival, we find our role,
With brimming joy and a twinkling soul.

The Sculptor of Fate

A chisel pranced with a cheeky grin,
Sculpting stories from the chaos within.
With every tap, a giggle rings,
As silly shapes take flight on wings.

In the studio of dreams, we spin,
Crafting laughter from tall tales and spins.
The clay of life, both messy and bright,
Molds the funny, our pure delight.

With a wink and a nudge, fate plays a tune,
Sculpting destiny beneath the moon.
Every blunder becomes a funny fate,
As we shape our journey, oh isn't it great?

So let's embrace this whimsical art,
With a joyful soul and an open heart.
For in the hands of the sculptor's game,
We become the silly, never the same.

Threading Through the Unknown

In a land where ideas take flight,
A needle danced in the moonlight.
It poked at clouds, made them sigh,
Crafting hats for the shy old guy.

A stitch here and a knot there,
We laughed till our cheeks were bare.
With every twist, a new tale spun,
Who knew fabric could be so much fun?

The fabric store's a whirlwind ride,
Where bolts of nonsense jump and hide.
Each thread a path, we giggle and weave,
In this tapestry, we surely believe.

So take your whims, and make them bold,
Add glitter and sparkles, let them unfold.
With each errant loop, we chuckle and cheer,
For the zany adventure is always near.

Bending Towards Dreams

A rubber band with lofty schemes,
Snapped at plans and wild dreams.
It stretched so far, then twanged with glee,
Launching ideas for all to see.

We bent the rules just for a laugh,
Messed up math, made rainbow graphs.
In a room full of giggles and quirks,
We plotted journeys through silly works.

Try to catch clouds with just one hand,
Dreams like jellybeans, unplanned.
The more we sipped on sweetened juice,
The crazier our goals became, loose.

With every leap into the air,
We somersaulted without a care.
Chasing the sun that danced and gleamed,
In our world of fun, all things seemed.

The Arrival of Tomorrow

A calendar flipped without a peep,
Tomorrow arrived while we were asleep.
It brought gifts wrapped in bright surprise,
Like socks that squeaked and dancing pies.

With time machines made of cardboard and tape,
We zoomed through places, oh what a shape!
Every misstep brought a hearty laugh,
Steering dreams on a curious path.

The clock ticked loudly, but we pressed on,
Painting the night till the morning dawn.
In the chaos, we found friendly giggles,
Time traveled whenever we jiggled.

So here's to the arrival we never sought,
Made of moments and quirky thought.
Tomorrow's antics, all out in stream,
Unravel life's most absurd dream.

Loops of Faith

Like spaghetti swirling in a bowl,
We twirled ideas, lost control.
Each noodle a whim, a silly thought,
We giggled at what we'd dared to plot.

A leap of truth from heights unreal,
Trusting the prop, our hearts would steal.
The jester spun as the crowd went wild,
With faith in laughter, like a carefree child.

In a world of noodles, we joined the dance,
Chasing each loop, daring chance.
With every twist, a chuckle grew,
In the spools of joy, we just flew.

So let's tie our dreams on a funny string,
In this circus of life, we'll flap and swing.
With every loop, a new song we'll sing,
In sticky moments, joy takes wing.

Twists in the Journey

A snail wore a hat, quite the sight,
It jogged on the path, oh what a fright!
With each tiny step, it shimmied with glee,
Who knew slow could dance, just like a spree?

A frog learned to sing, in a deep, croaky tone,
It startled the crickets, 'Get off my phone!'
With each ribbit it missed, a note flew out wide,
The crickets all laughed, but hoppin' with pride.

A turtle once painted, in colors so bright,
But slipped in a puddle, what a funny plight!
It called for a friend, "Help me out, oh dear!"
And out popped a duck, "At least it's not clear!"

As journeys unfold, with every odd twist,
The laughter we share, one thing that won't miss.
Life's twists and turns, never quite in line,
Can spark up the joy, oh how we dine!

Opening Chapters

In the library, cats read books upside down,
A tale of a king who lost his own crown.
He searched high and low, in the fridge, then the chair,
To find it again, needed help from a bear.

A mouse with a quill wrote a story so bold,
Of cheese he could eat, a plot he had unfold.
But halfway through dinner, he lost his own snack,
The cat looked quite pleased, 'Well, that's a way back!'

Those scribbles turned wild, as words filled the page,
Each laugh was a dance, an unwritten stage.
As the curtain pulled back on the turning of time,
Each chapter we wrote, was a giggle in rhyme.

The book ended sweet, with a party on toast,
With bread made of laughter, we all had to boast.
In opening lines, new tales come to play,
With every sharp twist, it brightens the day!

Unraveled Dreams

A dream in a cloud, said, 'I won't fly high,
I'd rather just sit and eat pie in the sky.'
But puffs of soft fluff, they giggled too loud,
So dreams that stay grounded, got lost in the crowd.

A dragon once snored, setting fires so bright,
He dreamed of being, a star in the night.
But woke up and sneezed, sent sparks through the air,
A comet flew by, 'Whoa! Look, that's not fair!'

A fish in the sea had ambitions so grand,
To join in a band, play the conch shell, and stand.
But tripped on a shell and sank down with a splash,
Now sells its CDs with a bubblegum bash!

In dreams where we laugh, the fun knows no end,
The twists that we take, we just gladly suspend.
With each little giggle, a tale weaves anew,
A tapestry of joy, shared by me and you!

Renewing the Fabric of Time

A clock wore a scarf, so stylish and neat,
With pendulum swings, it danced to the beat.
But when it took flight, round the room like a kite,
It tangled itself, oh, what a comical sight!

A time-traveling shoe, asked, 'Hey, where's my pair?'
It hopped through the ages, lost but with flair.
In medieval times, it found knights and a hat,
But forgot all the jokes from where it once sat.

A watch thought it'd age like a fine, dusty wine,
But missed all its appointments, oh such a decline!
As gears started rusting, it chuckled away,
In aging with laughter, it brightened the gray.

In this fabric of life, every thread holds a chuckle,
Each tick and each tock, makes us smile and buckle.
So, from every twist, we wear joy like a rhyme,
In moments repeated, we spin and unwind!

The Loom of Possibilities

In the attic of dreams, a party awaits,
Where mismatched socks dance and celebrate.
Weaving through laughter and threads spun high,
Even the buttons on shirts start to fly!

A spool of confusion rolls under the chair,
Chasing a rogue cat with a tangle of hair.
Knots in the fabric, oh what a delight,
Creating a quilt that shines ever so bright!

With every new pattern, my mind starts to twirl,
As I trip over stitches in this crazy world.
But who needs precision when joy's on the line?
Let the seams be crooked, I'll be just fine!

So here's to each twist and each silly turn,
In life's funny loom, there's so much to learn.
Amidst all the chaos, we'll dance and we'll play,
For the joys of the journey are never cliché!

Freshly Stitched Paths

With fabric in hand, I plot out new trails,
Buttons of fortune, embroidered with tales.
Zippers that giggle, seams that can sing,
Every misstep feels like a colorful fling!

Around every corner, surprises await,
A patchwork of joy, oh, isn't it great?
Snagging my sleeve on a doorknob so sly,
I wonder if this path leads up to the sky!

Strings that get tangled, a loop de loop dance,
Each stumble a chance for a whimsical chance.
Who knew the road could be stitched with such fun?
A tapestry spun under the bright golden sun!

So let's craft our journeys with laughter galore,
Chasing the shadows right out of the door.
Through crinkles and twists, I'll skip and I'll prance,
Life's a funny quilt – let's give it a chance!

Embracing Uncertainty

In the garden of life, we plant seeds of doubt,
Hoping they bloom, but not sure what's out.
A comedy sketch where the plot twists abound,
Wait, did that pumpkin just jump off the ground?

Wobbling with glee, we dance down the lane,
Wishing on stars, and they giggle in vain.
What if the flowers all laugh back in jest?
We'll wear all our quirks like a wacky old vest!

So here in this moment, we twirl without cares,
Collecting the chuckles like misfit souvenirs.
With every wrong turn, new adventures appear,
Embracing the chaos, let's toast with a cheer!

In the whirlwind of choice, let's kick off our shoes,
And leap into puddles of glitter and blues.
For in every quirk and silly mishap we find,
Lies the joy of the journey, where laughter is kind!

The Arc of Aspirations

With a swing and a sway, we reach for the stars,
Dodging the comets that dance with guitars.
Painting our hopes in the hues of delight,
As we juggle our dreams on this whimsical flight!

Every missed catch is a giggle released,
A jump from the high dive into the feast.
What's that? A rainbow? Let's slide down its tail,
Making memories fresh like a berry-filled pail!

The curve of our wishes bends laughter on cue,
When every mistake feels like something brand new.
So let's kite-fly our dreams, with no risk of fall,
For the arc of our hopes is the greatest of all!

So grab that big dream, and give it a whirl,
As we flip through the pages of life in a whirl.
In the laughter of aspirations, we find our rapport,
And paint our adventures forever-more!

Serendipity in Stitches

A crooked seam and a wild thread,
I stitched my dreams but woke instead.
Laughter echoes in a tangled fate,
Who knew a knot could be this great?

My fabric's patchwork tells a tale,
Of mismatched moments that never fail.
With each snip, I find a new start,
Sewing joy into every heart.

A button here, a hole in my shoe,
Who knew my wardrobe had such a view?
Each stitch a giggle, each rip a cheer,
I fashion my life, year after year!

So here's to the seams that twist and turn,
In this wacky dance, we always learn.
Serendipity in every thread,
Where laughter's the best kind of thread!

The Color of Revival

A splash of yellow, a dash of green,
Life's a palette, if you know what I mean.
Each morning's sunrise paints a new way,
Even the clouds giggle in dismay!

I tripped on rainbows and stumbled on cheer,
In every misstep, my wishes appear.
With every hue, let's dance in the sun,
In this colorful chaos, we have our fun!

The red of a blush on my friend's face,
Or the blue of a sky that we can't replace.
From drab to fab, we're painting it bright,
In this vibrant saga, we'll take flight!

So grab your brushes, let's mix and swirl,
In a canvas of laughter, we'll give it a whirl.
Revival in colors, each shade a delight,
Let's splash our joy with all of our might!

Fresh Threads in an Old Loom

An ancient loom with tales to weave,
Threads of the old trickle down like leaves.
With every pull, a giggle bends,
New yarns whisper where the old one ends.

Each loop a story, each knot a laugh,
Who thought life could be an artful craft?
In the tapestry, we find our place,
A dance of patterns, a cozy embrace.

Rip and tear, we patch with glee,
In this fabric of life, what will we see?
With fresh threads, we make it shine,
A chuckle here, a friendship line!

The weaver chuckles, the shuttle skips,
As the colors twirl in whimsical flips.
Old meets new in a funny parade,
Here's to the joy that we've made!

Awakening the Unwritten

A blank page waits with a cheeky grin,
Will it be a saga or a tale of kin?
With awkward scribbles and playful prose,
I tease out whispers as the laughter grows.

Each line a giggle, each word a dance,
As I fumble through this silly chance.
What plots await in my messy quill?
A romp through dreams, a whimsical thrill!

So grab your pens, don't let them rest,
In the realm of stories, we are blessed.
With every jot, laugh lines appear,
Awakening tales that we hold dear.

The unwritten awaits, let's scribble our cheer,
Life's a funny book, let's raise a beer!
In every chapter, let's spin and play,
For the unwritten yearns to see the day!

Loops of Hope

In a world of twinkling dreams,
Socks can vanish, or so it seems.
Pair them up, they start to dance,
Who knew laundry had romance?

With every twist and playful spin,
Life's a jigsaw—where to begin?
Don't fret over missing mates,
They're off on grand adventures, great!

Come on, let's all play the game,
Who needs perfection? It's all the same!
In knots and loops, we find our way,
Tangled laughs brighten the day.

The Tapestry of Tomorrow

A quilt of chaos, colorful threads,
Stitching dreams in silly spreads.
Tomorrow's plans wrapped tight in a bow,
Oh wait, that's last week's doughnut dough!

Woven wishes with a touch of glee,
Catch that squirrel; what will it be?
Excited, we'll jump, and then fall flat,
Who knew a trampoline was a welcome mat?

Messy fibers in a world askew,
Life's a patchwork, just like me and you.
Hold on tight, or you may slide,
Into laughter, along for the ride.

Threads of Promise

Spools of laughter roll down the street,
Snag those dreams; oh, what a feat!
Twist and twirl with utmost grace,
Hope's a game; it's all in the chase.

Unraveling tales with giggles and cheer,
Sewing seeds of joy, drawing near.
In tangled knots, we find the fun,
Who knew mischief was never done?

As needles pricked our daring fate,
Jump in the fabric, don't wait!
With threads of promise, we create,
A patch of joy—we celebrate!

Unfurling the Future

Wrapped in paper, surprises await,
Open it gently, don't tempt fate!
Each fold tickles with potential grand,
Future's a buffet; take a hand!

Wriggle and giggle as we explore,
Unroll the laughter; we all want more!
Pinch those dreams, don't let them slip,
Life's a rollercoaster, take a trip!

Hopes are balloons, let them fly high,
Dance in the wind, touch the sky.
Life's a party; come join the fun,
Unfurling joy; we've only just begun!

Ribbons of Reflection

Tying laughs with a bright string,
Old tales twist while new ones sing.
Giggles dance in the spring air,
A ribbon's pull leads to mischief's flair.

Mirror games with a bow in sight,
Catching glimmers of morning light.
Each twist and turn, a playful peek,
In knots of joy, we find our cheek.

Surprises hide beneath the sheen,
Who knew laughter was a routine?
Yet here we skip, chasing the dream,
In colorful threads, we gleam and beam.

Seizing the New Curve

Life's a ride on a wiggly line,
We zig and zag, feeling just fine.
With every swerve, a chuckle springs,
Bumping into joy, oh, the joy it brings!

Round the corner, what will we find?
A silly face or a jelly-bean mind?
Curves of fate with a giggling twist,
In every bend, a chance not to miss.

Riding the wave with silly hats,
Wacky antics and playful spats.
Life's curves unfold, a wild parade,
In laughter's arms, we're never afraid.

The Tangled Adventure

In a jungle of hearts, we roam and tangle,
With giggles and grins, our worries dangle.
From knots of humor, we find our way,
Untangling chaos in a comical play.

A cat with a bow and a dog in a hat,
Chasing wild dreams of where we're at.
Trip over laughter, oh, what a sight!
In every stumble, the mood feels just right.

Tangled in threads of joy and glee,
Every twist holds a mystery.
With each knot tied, we laugh, we cheer,
Ready for what's next, our paths are clear.

Sails of New Beginnings

Hoist up the sails on this ship of fun,
Waves of giggles will soon overrun.
With winds of whimsy, we take our flight,
Charting new courses under stars so bright.

Oars made of laughter, paddling through cheer,
In each splash of joy, a fresh new year.
We sail through storms with a wink and a wave,
Heartfelt moments our spirits will save.

Navigating life like an ocean of jest,
With friends at the helm, we're truly blessed.
In tides of happiness, forever we'll roam,
With sails unfurled, we've found our home.

Whispers in the Wind

A gust tickles the trees with glee,
As squirrels chat about their spree.
Leaves dance like they've had a drink,
While pigeons plot over a missing link.

The clouds gossip on a lazy day,
While bees buzz in a comic play.
Sun rays giggle, peek and hide,
Nature's punchlines, none can decide.

A butterfly trips, oh what a sight,
Wings flapping with all its might.
It pirouettes and collides, whoops!
With flowers dressed in jubilant loops.

So take a moment, let out a laugh,
As nature sketches its crafty path.
In every whisper, joy is found,
In the playful dance all around.

The First Curve

At the mountain's start, just beyond the bend,
A goat practices a new trend.
With a hop and skip, it goes for gold,
While the trees watch on, feeling bold.

A snail slides down the winding hill,
While critters gather, their hearts to fill.
Each twist and turn brings joy anew,
As the path unfolds, not one but a few.

A rabbit's bold leap catches the air,
While tortoises murmur, 'Life's not a pair!'
With silly grins, they all engage,
In this playful dance, life's a stage.

So let's embrace the first slight turn,
Where laughter and joy so brightly burn.
In life's adventures, curveballs are fun,
Just like a race where all can run.

Knotted Dreams

With yarn in hand, I start to weave,
A tapestry of things to believe.
Each loop and twist, a story spun,
Where laughter and fun can't be outdone.

The light bulb flickers, ideas collide,
As my cat pounces with fervent pride.
An unexpected tangle, a thread gone rogue,
Yet here comes a smile, it's on the log!

Friends gathered round for a knot-tying spree,
As laughter echoes, filling with glee.
We pull, we yank, the yarn doesn't care,
And soon we're all caught in a colorful snare.

So here's to the dreams that twist and bind,
Where hilarity and joy intertwine.
In messy creations, let's find our way,
For every knotted tale has its play.

Embroidered Intentions

With needles flashing, I start my quest,
To stitch up some fun, I am truly blessed.
Each thread a giggle, each knot a cheer,
As patterns emerge, bringing joy near.

While sewing, I notice a curious ant,
Wearing a hat, oh how gallant!
It dances around like it owns the place,
In my crafting corner, it's leading the race.

A splash of colors, a mishap occurs,
As the cat pounces, oh how it stirs!
A fabric whirlwind, like chaos unleashed,
Yet laughter erupts, like a glorious feast.

So bring forth your stitches, your snips, your thread,
As we plot and plan, let silliness spread.
With intentions so bright, let our hearts sing,
In the fabric of laughter, joy is the king!

Fresh String on a Quiet Night

In the still of the air, a string is tight,
A cat walks by, all stealth and slight.
It pounces with flair, but misses the mark,
A tumble and roll, a hilarious lark.

The night is alive with the echoes of fun,
Where shadows are chasing, and laughter has spun.
A raccoon peeks out, wearing a grin,
It's ready to join in, let the antics begin!

Up in the trees, the branches sway low,
A squirrel does a dance, putting on quite a show.
With a flick of its tail and a twist in its leap,
It makes us all chuckle, but still, we can't sleep.

And so in the quiet, new tales slowly bloom,
With mischief afoot in the light of the moon.
Each twist and each turn brings a snicker or two,
In this world of delight, let the funness ensue!

Twists of Fate

In the tangled threads of unplanned schemes,
A baker forgot sugar, or so it seems.
The pastries were bland, a comical sight,
But the townsfolk just laughed, oh what a night!

A dog made a dash with a sock in its mouth,
It raced through the park, headed south then north.
With people in tow, they ran in delight,
Chasing that pup till they fell in a fright!

A kite took a journey, caught up in a tree,
Holding onto dreams with fervor and glee.
The owner just sighed, another failed flight,
But the laughter it sparked was pure, and just right.

With each twist and turn, life throws us a curve,
Our fumbles and stumbles are things we deserve.
Embrace every mishap and find joy in the chase,
For in every misstep, there's magic in space!

The Tender Arc

On a sunny day, a child looks up high,
With a grin on their face, and dreams in the sky.
A paper plane flies, but just takes a dive,
Even when it flops, oh, how it feels alive!

The swing set creaks as it goes to and fro,
A friendly little ghost decides to show.
With arms outstretched, it gives one big push,
Sending all laughter in a whoosh and a whoosh!

A rubber band snaps, chaos on a shelf,
A stack of old books said, "You need help!"
Yet giggles erupt; such a splendid spree,
In the arc of each moment, we feel so carefree.

In the tender grace of life's playful embrace,
We find the delight in each silly chase.
So let the arcs form, let the laughter take flight,
In the heart of this world, everything feels right!

Launching into the Blue

A rocket made of cardboard, ready to soar,
With crayons and laughter, it opens the door.
"Five, four, three," counts a child with glee,
Then it tips on its side, oh, where could it be?

The cat takes a leap, a daring escape,
In pursuit of the launch pad, creating a shape.
With a leap and a bound, it lands in a plume,
Bouncing around like, "I love this room!"

A bucket of water, a splash and a cheer,
The dog dives right in, with no hint of fear.
Soaking wet friends now all sing a new tune,
As water balloons fly, who cares for the moon?

From rockets to pets, the laughter takes flight,
Each splash is a mission, oh what pure delight.
With dreams in our hearts and a grin on our face,
We're launching together, embracing the space!

The Quiet Ties of Morning

In the dawn, a cat stretches wide,
While the coffee pots dance with pride.
A toaster pops like a festive tune,
As socks have a party, by the light of the moon.

Muffins tumble, a soft little race,
They're racing to meet a buttered embrace.
But wait! The jam's lost in a jelly fight,
With breakfast chaos, oh what a sight!

The chair squeaks soft with a giggly cheer,
As the sun peeks in, bringing good cheer.
Pajamas are heroes in their lazy quest,
While the clock rolls its eyes and takes a rest.

So here's to mornings, both wild and bright,
Where mishaps and laughter unite to ignite.
Gather your joys, let chaos ignite,
In the kitchen of whims, oh what a delight!

A Brush with Destiny

In a shop where colors clash and play,
A bucket of paint steals the day.
The canvas rolls over, shakes it off,
While the brushes conspire, giggle and scoff.

One splash of blue does a tango so grand,
While yellow and green form a funky band.
But oh! A misstep sends red on a spree,
It leaves little handprints, oh woe is he!

With every stroke, chaos reigns supreme,
Creating a masterpiece that's more like a dream.
But will it be framed or thrown out the door?
The artist shrugs, and giggles galore!

So grab your colors, just wild and free,
As laughter and paint dance in glee.
In the artworks of life, don't take it too hard,
For mishaps create joy, every single shard!

The Cascading Flow

Waterfalls giggle as they tumble down,
While ducks wear their finest, a quacking crown.
They splash and they dive, oh what a scene,
In this riot of joy, no one's too keen!

With rainbows above bringing optical cheers,
The sun peeks out; it conquers the fears.
A boat made of paper drifts down the stream,
While fish blow bubbles in a playful dream.

But wait! A frog leaps—a splash and a croak,
He lands in the boat with a laugh and a poke.
The paper ship wobbles, then swirls with delight,
As the frog shouts, "This is quite the fright!"

So journey along with laughter and flow,
For the waters of life have much more to show.
In chaos, there's joy, and in laughter, there's grace,
Even frogs in a boat find their perfect place!

Shadows of Untamed Paths

In the forest where shadows play hide-and-seek,
A squirrel in glasses looks quite unique.
With berries in tow, he ambles around,
In search of mischief, he's wildly profound.

A branch snaps and echoes like a loud joke,
It starts off a dance with a nearby oak.
The leaves laugh so hard they can hardly stay,
As critters join in for an impromptu play.

A path twists and turns like a rubbery dream,
With shadows that giggle and sway with a gleam.
But watch for the puddles, they leap and they splash,
With a clown-fish in tow, causing quite the crash!

So wander these woods with a skip in your step,
Where shadows and laughter in chaos adept.
Each twist is a chuckle, each turn a delight,
With untamed paths showing humor so bright!

Halo of New Starts

In the land of quirky dreams,
A chicken crossed the street to scheme.
With feathers bright and clucking flair,
It sought a new life, free of care.

Wobbling on its neon shoes,
It jived along with laughing roos.
Each step a giggle, each turn a twist,
In the chaos, it found joy to persist.

Outrageous tales spread like fire,
Of clucking dancers, raising choir.
The road ahead was paved with glee,
A feathered legend, wild and free.

So here's to fresh starts, wild and wise,
With jokes and laughter, reach for the skies.
One silly chicken, taking on fate,
With humor and joy, don't hesitate!

The Unfolding Arc

A rubber band stretched too tight,
Twanged back with a comical bite.
It wasn't just elastic, it had flair,
Bringing giggles, bouncing everywhere.

With each release, it flew through air,
Knocking over cupcakes with a daring glare.
A party trick gone hilariously wrong,
The birthday song now a bouncy throng.

Twists and turns, what a wild ride,
The rubber band, oh, what a guide!
In this wacky arc, we learn to laugh,
While dodging icing, half a cupcake half.

So let's embrace the zany path
Where laughter reigns, and fun is the math.
In every twist, a joke unfolds,
In this arc of life, pure delight holds!

Embrace of Fresh Paths

A squirrel on a skateboard, oh what a sight,
Trying to outrun its dreams in the night.
With acorns flinging in every direction,
It skidded past trees, a furry perfection.

Balancing on wheels, a leap and a twirl,
The forest erupted in laughter and whirl.
As branches swayed to the squirrel's delight,
Every tumble was grace, a quirky flight.

Cheering woodland friends gathered 'round,
As nutty antics made laughter abound.
With each new path, a chuckle grew loud,
For every misstep, the critter was proud.

So let's take a cue from this tiny ace,
And skateboard through life with a smile on our face.
When we embrace the odd trails we find,
We discover the giggles that life leaves behind!

Knots of Hope

In a garden of shoelaces, tangled and sweet,
A snail tied a knot, truly hard to beat.
It wriggled and wobbled, determined in fate,
Turning snafus into something first-rate.

With ribbons and bows, the snail took a stand,
Decorating flowers, a glimmering band.
It laughed at the chaos, the twists and the ties,
For playtime was magic in disguise!

In the mess of the world, let dreams intertwine,
A knot is just wiggles that choose to align.
With hope as our thread, let's weave through the day,
Finding giggles in knots along the way.

So here's to the twists that life has in store,
With laughter in every dilemma we explore.
In the big bowl of humor, let's stir with a glee,
For the tightest of knots can set laughter free!

The Echo of a New Path

In a forest of shoes, they dance and prance,
Worn by those who sought romance.
Each step a giggle, each turn a cheer,
Whispers of journeys that draw us near.

A squirrel with a hat tips his brim,
As hedgehogs play hide and seek on a whim.
The rabbit wears goggles, ready to dive,
On this silly quest, we feel so alive.

The map is a doodle, a scribble of dreams,
With arrows that wiggle and silly seams.
A treasure marked 'X' with pie and ice cream,
In the echoing woods, we laugh and we beam.

So follow the laughter, the cheer in the air,
A path paved with giggles, we'll go anywhere.
With shoes full of joy, we wander along,
In this funny tale, we all belong.

The Harmonies of What Awaits

Cats in top hats, serenade the moon,
While frogs in the pond hum an old tune.
The stars look down with twinkling eyes,
As the world dances under the night skies.

Llamas on stilts strut with pride,
Balancing dreams on a joy-filled ride.
Their laughter echoes, a comical refrain,
As we twirl and spin in the light summer rain.

A ukulele plays a silly beat,
As otters all gather for a boisterous feat.
Together we sing of all that's ahead,
With whimsy and wonder, our hearts full of bread.

So join in the fun, let your spirit ignite,
In this wacky world, everything feels right.
With joy in our steps and smiles so bright,
Life's jolly symphony invites us to flight.

Ties of Dawn

The sun peeks over with a jolly grin,
Caffeine-fueled gnomes start their day with a spin.
Muffins frolic as the kettle sings,
In this breakfast tale, joy is the king.

Raccoons in pajamas do the cha-cha,
While pancakes perform a flip, ha-ha-ha!
Syrup rivers flow, sweet and wide,
As platypuses waddle, full of pride.

The toast pops up with a jubilant cheer,
Spreading jam like confetti, oh so near!
Each little moment a giggle, a tease,
As dawn ties us up in a warm, silly breeze.

So embrace the dawn with laughter, not frowns,
For each sunrise brings new silly crowns.
With breakfast best friends, we start our day,
In ties of delight, let's dance and play!

Gift Wrapping Promises

Packages bouncing with giggles inside,
Unwrapping laughter, joy can't hide.
The paper's a maze, ribbons twist and twine,
Each fold a secret, each crease a sign.

Cats sneak peeks with wide, curious eyes,
While dogs doze off, dreaming of pies.
The gifts bring grins and silly surprises,
With hats made of laughter, joy never disguises.

As we rip through the layers and celebrate fun,
Every reveal has us laughing, oh what a run!
From goofy trinkets to things that make sense,
Each present a promise of joy that's immense.

So gather your friends for this jolly parade,
With gifts full of giggles, dreams that won't fade.
As we wrap up the moments with love and delight,
In this silly gifting, we soar to new heights.

The Start of Something Bright

In a world full of chances, we trip and we roll,
A tumble can spark the most vibrant goal.
With chuckles and glances, we wobble and sway,
Who knew silly stumbles would brighten the day?

From flops to great finds, it's all in the jest,
We chase after dreams, never feeling the rest.
With laughter as fuel, we leap with delight,
In the chaos of life, we're dancing in flight.

Each mishap a treasure, a jewel in disguise,
We giggle through hiccups, embrace every surprise.
So let's raise a toast to our cartoonish spree,
For what's life without laughter, wild and free?

With each quirky twist, a new door can swing,
Finding joy in the silly is our favorite thing.
Let's wander and wonder, with spirits so light,
Here's to the dance where we start something bright!

Flowing Ribbons in the Wind

Tangled in laughter, the streamers take flight,
Swirling with whimsy, a colorful sight.
We run through the park, ribbons waving just so,
As if they're our tails, we're putting on a show.

With giggles and gasps, we trip on our lace,
Each stumble unwinds with a hilarious grace.
The wind whispers secrets, we chase after dreams,
Twirling and whirling, we savor the screams.

Like a game of tag with the breeze and the sun,
Our hearts race with joy; we're just having fun.
Let's catch the soft clouds, we'll skip like a stone,
In a world full of laughter, we're never alone.

So let's ride the currents, these ribbons of glee,
Boundless adventures, just you and me.
With each twist of fate, joy's never too far,
In the dance of the ribbons, we shine just like stars!

The Crescent Approach

A bright cheeky moon in his crescent-shaped grin,
Winks at the world, letting mischief begin.
We stumble through shadows, giggling with ease,
Chasing our dreams like leaves in the breeze.

With each joyful flip, we defy every rule,
Just a pair of odd ducks who've lost their cool.
We paddle through puddles, we shout at the stars,
Creating our magic, no matter how far.

So here's to the night and its whimsical hue,
Every star is a guide that leads us anew.
With laughter our compass, we'll shine in the dark,
In the crescent's embrace, we ignite our spark!

Through the laughter and light, we sketch out our fate,
In the rich tapestry, it's never too late.
With each little giggle, our hearts start to rhyme,
In the dance of the crescent, we're having a time!

Tethered Journeys

We're tethered together, like kites on a line,
Each dip and each lift is a moment divine.
With giggles and gaffes, we soar and we sway,
On a journey of laughter, forever at play.

With fumbles and blunders, we dance through the fray,
Every bump on the road gives new roles to our sway.
Like balloons at a party, we rise with great zest,
Through the highs and the lows, it's a quirk at its best.

Silly setbacks become our best tales to tell,
We spin round and round, like a carousel.
With our hearts intertwined, we're ready to roam,
In this laughter-filled flight, we find our true home.

So here's to the journeys that make us feel bright,
In the dance of the tethered, we take off in flight.
With laughter our anchor, we're free as the breeze,
On this merry adventure, we do just as we please!

Freshly Woven Journeys

In a world that's spun like yarn,
We stumble and trip, yet never quite mourn.
Knots in our plans, we dance and we sway,
With laughter we start, come what may.

The map's upside down, roads lead to the sky,
Who needs a GPS? We'll just wing and fly.
Every turn a surprise, like pie on the face,
Our travel's a circus, a joyful chase.

Oops! There goes a shoe in the mix,
But do we complain? Nah, it's just our tricks.
With each silly mishap, the journey unfolds,
In absurdity's grasp, adventure beholds.

So here's to the trail, with twists that delight,
We'll navigate chaos with giggles in sight.
With every misstep, we're learning to cheer,
Life's a grand tour, let's toast with good beer!

The Spark of Potential

In a kitchen of dreams, the pot's boiling hot,
We whip up our hopes with a sprinkle, a plot.
A dash of the awkward, a splash of the fun,
With ingredients mixed, our laughter's begun.

Ideas like popcorn, they pop and they fly,
Some stick to the ceiling, oh my oh my!
Yet every explosion reveals something grand,
In the mess, we discover the magic we planned.

With schemes in a blender, we whirl and we blend,
Each flavor a tune, on which we depend.
So here's to the strange and the wild, oh dear,
Our potential's a party, let's all grab a beer!

We'll juggle our goals like a clown on a ball,
In a circus of hopes, we will not let them fall.
For in the making, the smiles will dispense,
Life's a comedy show, with joy as the suspense!

Gentle Twists of Fate

Like twisting a pretzel, life ties us in knots,
But laughter's the key to unravel our thoughts.
With every odd turn, and giggle or sigh,
We embrace the absurdity, give it a try.

While fate plays its tricks, with a grin on its face,
We dance on the edge of a wild, silly space.
Each twist is a giggle, each bend is a rhyme,
Our fate's just a prank, and we're having a time.

So here's to the moments that catch us off guard,
With fate as the joker, we'll laugh, we'll discard.
In the game of the silly, we're all on the stage,
Turning fate into punchlines, released from the cage.

With hearts full of joy, and smiles at the gate,
We welcome the whims, and we'll never be late.
For in every twist, we'll find treasures await,
In the dance of surprises, our lives are first-rate!

A Song of Loosening

The ties that we tighten are fun for a while,
But loosen their grip, and life's worth a smile.
Like fidgeting children, we break from constraint,
With antics that make even seriousness faint.

A bow with a flurry, it slips and it flies,
As we tumble and laugh, beneath sunny skies.
Who knew a loose thread could unravel such cheer?
In the silly unfurling, our joys reappear.

So let down your guard and give life a twirl,
A dance of forgetfulness, wit in a whirl.
We'll sing out our freedom with giggles and glee,
In the chorus of laughter, come loosen with me!

With each strand unbound, we become quite the show,
In the playful expanse, let your colors flow.
For in the loosening, we find our own song,
Life's a funny journey; let's all sing along!

www.ingramcontent.com/pod-product-compliance
Lightning Source LLC
Chambersburg PA
CBHW070308120526
44590CB00017B/2591